THE **BIG BOOK** OF
Dad Jokes

800 Unbearable, Groan-Inducing One-Liners, Puns, and **Riddles** to Make You the **King** of Subpar Comedy

Joe Kerz

Racehorse Publishing

Copyright © 2022 by Racehorse Publishing

Racehorse Publishing books may be purchased in bulk at special discounts for sales promotion, corporate gifts, fund-raising, or educational purposes. Special editions can also be created to specifications. For details, contact the Special Sales Department, Skyhorse Publishing, 307 West 36th Street, 11th Floor, New York, NY 10018 or info@skyhorsepublishing.com.

Racehorse Publishing™ is a pending trademark of Skyhorse Publishing, Inc.®, a Delaware corporation.

Visit our website at www.skyhorsepublishing.com.

10 9 8 7 6 5 4 3

Library of Congress Cataloging-in-Publication Data is available on file.

Cover design by Kai Texel
Cover illustration by Getty Images
Interior art by iStockphoto

ISBN: 978-1-63158-662-0
E-Book ISBN: 978-1-63158-665-1

Printed in the United States of America

Portions of the book were previously published as
Dad Jokes (ISBN: 978-1-63158-372-8) and
Really Bad Dad Jokes (ISBN: 978-1-63158-513-5)

INTRODUCTION

Fatherhood is never easy. Try as you might to be there for your kids, you won't always succeed. However, they can always count on you to be there with the dad's most useful tool: the Dad Joke! *Dad Jokes* can always be used to embarrass and antagonize your children, eliciting the classic eye-roll, face-palm, and the occasional exclamation of "DAD!"—after all, isn't it a dad's main purpose in life to torment their children with puns in public?

Whether you're an expert pun-maker or a novice, you'll never run out of embarrassing riddles and puns with *The Big Book of Dad Jokes*! This compendium of the most groan-worthy jokes and one-liners will be sure to induce the reactions that you live for (even though they make your children die a little inside). Be prepared for any and every situation with a handy quip. Passing by a graveyard? I bet people are just dying to get in! Having pizza for dinner? Never mind . . . those jokes are just too *cheesy*. You'll never run out of opportunities to make your family wish they'd just left you at home!

So, grab your goggles and swim trunks and dive on into this book that's perfect for any father, young or old! You'll learn everything you need to know about mastering the art of the Dad Joke and unleashing your embarassing humor upon your family and the world.

JOKES

1

WHAT DID THE POLICEMAN SAY TO HIS BELLY BUTTON?

You're under a vest!

2

Why did the cookie go to the hospital?

Because he felt crummy!

❸

Why did Billy throw the clock out of the window?

Because he wanted to see time fly!

❹

WHAT DO LAWYERS WEAR TO COURT?

Lawsuits!

❺

What do you call a fake noodle?

An impasta!

6

Why did the robber take a bath?

Because he wanted to make a clean getaway!

7

What did one toilet say to the other toilet?

You look flushed!

8

WHAT DO YOU CALL A BELT WITH A WATCH ON IT?

A waist of time!

9

How do you find a Princess?

You follow the foot Prince.

10

What lights up a soccer stadium?

A soccer match!

11

Where do snowmen keep their money?

In snow banks!

12

WHY SHOULDN'T YOU WRITE WITH A BROKEN PENCIL?

Because it's pointless!

13

Why did the man put his money in the freezer?

He wanted cold hard cash!

14

What lies at the bottom of the ocean and twitches?

A nervous wreck!

HOW DO YOU MAKE A TISSUE DANCE?

Put a little boogey in it!

What do you call a sleeping bull?

A bulldozer!

Why was the student's report card wet?

It was below C level!

Why wouldn't the shrimp share his treasure?

Because he was a little shellfish!

What do you call bears with no ears?

B.

20

What did the judge say when the skunk walked in the court room?

Odor in the court.

21

HOW MANY TICKLES DOES IT TAKE TO MAKE AN OCTOPUS LAUGH?

Ten-tickles.

22

What do you call the heavy breathing someone makes while trying to hold a yoga pose?

Yoga pants.

WHAT IS THE BEST DAY TO GO TO THE BEACH?

Sunday, of course!

How do hens cheer for their team?

They egg them on!

Why did the man with one hand cross the road?

To get to the second-hand shop.

26

WHEN DOES FRIDAY COME BEFORE THURSDAY?

In the dictionary!

27

How does NASA organize a party?

They planet.

28

What bow can't be tied?

A rainbow!

29

Why did the birdie go to the hospital?

To get a tweetment.

30

What has one head, one foot, and four legs?

A Bed.

31

Where did the computer go to dance?

To a disc-o.

32

WHY DID THE BANANA GO TO THE DOCTOR?

Because it was not peeling well.

33

Why is England the wettest country?

Because the queen has reigned there for years!

34

Why did the computer go to the doctor?

Because it had a virus!

35

Why did Roger go out with a prune?

Because he couldn't find a date!

36

What happened to the dog that swallowed a firefly?

It barked with de-light!

37

WHO EARNS A LIVING DRIVING THEIR CUSTOMERS AWAY?

A taxi driver.

HOW DO YOU SHOOT A KILLER BEE?

With a bee-bee gun.

Did you hear about the restaurant on the moon?

Great food, no atmosphere!

Want to hear a joke about paper?

Nevermind, it's tearable.

Why did the coffee file a police report?

It got mugged.

What do you call an elephant that doesn't

matter?

An irrelephant.

WHY DON'T SKELETONS EVER GO TRICK OR TREATING?

Because they have no body to go with.

44

**What did one snowman say to
the other one?**

Do you smell carrots?

45

**Did you hear about the man who
stole a calendar?**

He got 12 months.

46

**Where can you get chicken broth
in bulk?**

The Stock Market.

47

**What do you call a man with no nose
and no body?**

Nobody nose.

48

HOW MUCH DOES A
HIPSTER WEIGH?

An Instagram.

49

**What did the daddy tomato say to
the baby tomato?**

Catch up!

50

WHAT'S FORREST GUMP'S PASSWORD?

1forrest1.

51

Why did the scarecrow win an award?

Because he was outstanding in his field.

52

Why shouldn't you buy anything with Velcro on it?

It's a total rip-off!

What did Winnie The Pooh say to his agent?

Show me the honey!

What goes through towns, up and over hills, but doesn't move?

The road!

What kind of dogs like car racing?

Lap dogs.

56

Why was there thunder and lightning

in the lab?

The scientists were brainstorming!

WHY COULDN'T THE PIRATE PLAY CARDS?

Because he was sitting on the deck!

58

WHAT DO YOU CALL A BABY MONKEY?

A chimp off the old block.

59

Where do bees go to the bathroom?

At the BP station!

60

What did the blanket say to the bed?

Don't worry, I've got you covered!

Why did the traffic light turn red?

You would too if you had to change in the middle of the street!

What did one elevator say to the other elevator?

I think I'm coming down with something!

What do you get when you cross fish and an elephant?

Swimming trunks.

64

WHAT DO CALL CHEESE THAT ISN'T YOURS?

Nacho Cheese!

65

What kind of bird sticks to sweaters?

A Vel-Crow.

66

What washes up on very small beaches?

Microwaves.

67

WHAT KIND OF CRACKERS DO FIREMEN LIKE IN THEIR SOUP?

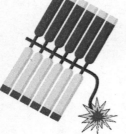

Firecrackers!

68

What did the digital clock say to the

grandfather clock?

Look grandpa, no hands!

69

What is an astronaut's favorite place on a computer?

The space bar!

70

Which month do soldiers hate most?

The month of March!

71

What did the judge say to the dentist?

Do you swear to pull the tooth, the whole tooth, and nothing but the tooth?

72

What starts with a P, ends with an E, and has a million letters in it?

Post Office!

73

WHICH U.S. STATE HAS THE SMALLEST SOFT DRINKS?

Mini-soda.

74

Why did the stadium get hot after the game?

All of the fans left.

75

WHAT DID THE DUCK SAY TO THE BARTENDER?

Put it on my bill.

76

How does a squid go into battle?

Well-armed.

77

What kind of tea is hard to swallow?

Reality.

78

Why was the guy looking for fast food on his friend?

Because his friend said dinner is on me.

79

What did the time traveler do when he was still hungry after his last bite?

He went back four seconds.

80

What do you call an unpredictable, out-of-control photographer?

A loose Canon.

81

DID YOU HEAR ABOUT THE SENSITIVE BURGLAR?

He takes things personally.

82

Did the disappointed smoker get everything he wanted for Christmas?

Clothes, but no cigar.

83

What do you call the sound a dog makes when it's choking on a piece of its owner's jewelry?

A diamond in the ruff.

WHY DID THE YOGURT GO TO THE ART EXHIBIT?

Because it was cultured.

Where do cows hang their paintings?

In the mooo-seum.

WHY DID THE TOMATO TURN RED?

Because it saw the salad dressing!

Why did the can crusher quit his job?

Because it was soda pressing.

What do bees do if they want to use public transport?

Wait at a buzz stop!

89

What did the fashion police officer say to his sweater?

"Do you know why I pulled you over?"

90

WHAT'S THE MOST MUSICAL PART OF A CHICKEN?

The drumstick.

91

Why was the baby strawberry crying?

Because his mom and dad were in a jam!

92

What did the fisherman say to the magician?

Pick a cod, any cod!

93

What did the red light say

to the green light?

Don't look, I'm changing!

94

Why couldn't the sesame seed leave the

casino?

Because he was on a roll.

95

What would Bears be without Bees?

Ears.

96

Why did the poor man sell yeast?

To raise some dough.

97

HOW DO SNAILS FIGHT?

They slug it out.

98

Why do bananas wear suntan lotion?

Because they peel.

99

What's the difference between ignorance and apathy?

I don't know and I don't care.

100

WHY ARE PENGUINS SOCIALLY AWKWARD?

Because they can't break the ice.

101

Where do hamburgers go to dance?

They go to the meat-ball.

102

WHAT KIND OF SHOES DO ALL SPIES WEAR?

Sneakers.

103

Why did the boy tiptoe past the medicine cabinet?

He didn't want to wake the sleeping pills!

What do you get when you put
your radio in the fridge?

Cool music.

Why did the belt go to jail?

Because it held up a pair of pants!

106

What do you call a bear with no socks on?

Bare-foot.

107

WHAT CAN YOU SERVE BUT NEVER EAT?

A volleyball.

108

Why did the boy sprinkle sugar on his pillow before he went to sleep?

So he could have sweet dreams.

109

What did the penny say to the other penny?

We make perfect cents.

Why did the hipster burn his tongue with his pizza?

He ate it before it was cool!

How do crazy people go through the forest?

They take the psycho path.

What do you call an apology written in dots and dashes?

Remorse code.

WHAT DO YOU CALL A FAT PSYCHIC?

A four-chin teller.

WHY AREN'T KOALAS ACTUAL BEARS?

The don't meet the koalafications.

What's brown and sticky?

A stick.

116

What's a foot long and slippery?

A slipper.

117

What's red and moves up and down?

A tomato in an elevator.

118

What do Alexander the Great and Winnie the Pooh have in common?

Same middle name.

Who walks into a restaurant, eats shoots and leaves?

A Panda.

WHAT DID ONE EYE SAY TO THE OTHER EYE?

Don't look now, but something between us smells.

What streets do ghosts haunt?

Dead ends!

WHAT DO YOU CALL IT WHEN BATMAN SKIPS CHURCH?

Christian Bale.

What did the grape do when it got stepped on?

It let out a little wine!

What did the time traveler do when he was still hungry after dinner?

He went back four seconds.

How many lips does a flower have?

Tu-lips.

What do you call a shoe made out of a banana?

A slipper.

WHY COULDN'T THE TOILET PAPER CROSS THE ROAD?

Because it got stuck in a crack.

128

How much does a pirate pay for corn?

A buccaneer.

129

What did the mayonnaise say when the refrigerator door was opened?

Close the door, I'm dressing.

130

How do you stop a bull from charging?

Cancel its credit card.

What's a skeleton's favorite musical instrument?

The trom-bone.

What disease do you get when you put up the Christmas decorations?

Tinselitus.

HOW DO BILLBOARDS TALK?

Sign language.

What do you get when you cross a snowman

with a vampire?

Frostbite.

Why was the sand wet?

Because the sea weed.

HOW DID THE BARBER
WIN THE RACE?

He knew a short cut.

137

What's orange and sounds like a parrot?

A carrot.

138

When is a door not a door?

When it's ajar.

139

WHY IS CORN SUCH A GOOD LISTENER?

Because it's all ears.

140

What do you call a pile of cats?

A meow-ntain.

141

Why did the golfer wear two pairs of pants?

In case he got a hole in one.

142

Why did the chicken cross the playground?

To get to the other slide.

143

What did the first plate say to the second plate?

Dinner's on me.

144

What did the football coach say to the broken vending machine?

Give me my quarterback.

145

WHY CAN'T YOU TRUST THE KING OF THE JUNGLE?

Because he's always lion.

146

WHEN IS A CAR NOT A CAR?

When it turns into a street.

147

How does a rancher keep track of his cattle?

With a cow-culator.

148

Have you heard about the pregnant bed bug?

She's going to have her baby in the spring.

149

What do you call a sleeping bull?

A bull-dozer.

150

Why is there a wall around the cemetery?

Because people are dying to get in.

151

Why could the bee not hear what people were saying?

He had wax in his ears.

152

WHAT'S E.T. SHORT FOR?

He's got little legs.

153

How do you make a Swiss roll?

Push him down a mountain.

154

What did the swordfish say to the marlin?

You're looking sharp.

155

WHAT DO OLYMPIC SPRINTERS EAT BEFORE A RACE?

Nothing. They fast.

156

What's a didgeridoo?

Whatever it wants to.

157

Did you hear about the sensitive burglar?

He takes things personally.

158

Why do cows wear bells?

Because their horns don't work.

159

How do you stop moles from digging in your garden?

Hide the spade.

160

DID YOU HEAR ABOUT THE ITALIAN CHEF WHO DIED.

He pasta way.

What does a nut say when it sneezes?

Cashew.

Why did Santa study music at college?

To improve his rapping skills.

How do you make a Venetian blind?

Poke him in the eyes.

164

WHAT DO YOU CALL CRYSTAL CLEAR URINE?

1080pee.

165

What do you call a group of disorganized cats?

A cat-astrophe.

166

WHY SHOULDN'T YOU PLAY CARDS ON THE SAVANNAH?

Because of all the cheetahs.

167

Did you hear about the population of Ireland's capital?

It's Dublin.

168

How do you impress a female baker?

Bring her flours.

169

Why did the bicycle fall over?

Because it was two tired.

170

Why did the mobile phone need glasses?

It lost all its contacts.

171

What did the hat say to the scarf?

You go ahead, I'll hang around.

172

WHAT DID THE BABY CORN SAY TO THE MAMA CORN?

Where's pop corn?

173

What did the chip say when he saw

the cheese stealing?

Hey, that's Nachos.

174

WHAT DO YOU CALL A BOAT WITH A HOLE IN THE BOTTOM?

A sink.

175

Why do seagulls fly over the sea?

Because if they flew over the bay they'd

be called bagels.

176

What kind of music do mummies listen to?

Wrap music.

177

Why did the cookie go to the doctors?

Because he felt crummy.

178

Why did the stadium get hot after the game?

All the fans left.

179

Why do bananas wear sunscreen?

To stop them from peeling.

180

What's the difference between America and a memory stick?

One's USA and the other's USB.

181

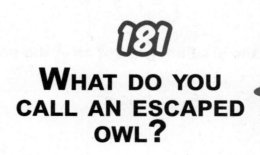

WHAT DO YOU CALL AN ESCAPED OWL?

Hoodini.

WHAT DID THE BIG CHIMNEY SAY TO THE LITTLE CHIMNEY?

You're too young to smoke.

What's a bear with no teeth called?

A gummy bear.

Why couldn't the bad sailor learn his alphabet?

Because he always got lost at C.

185

What did the first street say to the second street?

I'll meet you at the intersection.

186

Why are teddy bears never hungry?

Because they're always stuffed.

187

What did one toilet say to the other toilet?

You look flushed.

188

WHAT'S THE BEST TIME TO GO TO THE DENTIST?

Tooth hurty.

189

What do you call a factory that makes good products?

A satis-factory.

190

WHICH SIDE OF A DUCK HAS THE MOST FEATHERS?

The outside.

Where do Volkswagens go when they get old?

The old Volks home.

I went into a pet shop and asked for twelve bees. The shopkeeper counted out thirteen and handed them over.

"You've given me one too many."

"That one is a freebie."

What is it called when a pig loses its memory?

Hamnesia.

194

Three guys on a boat have four cigarettes but nothing to light them with.

So, they throw one cigarette overboard and the boat becomes a cigarette lighter.

195

What do elves rely on during political campaigns?

Propagandalf.

196

WHAT DID THE GOAT CHEESE SAY WHEN IT SAW ITSELF IN THE MIRROR?

"Haloomi!"

197

What do you call James Bond in a jacuzzi?

Bubble-0 Seven.

198

Bad puns are how eye roll.

199

WHAT DO YOU CALL A GROUP OF MUSICAL WHALES?

An orca-stra.

200

What do you get when you play tug of war

with a pig?

Pulled pork.

201

What do a dog and a phone have in common?

They both have collar ID.

202

What did the red light say to the green light?

Don't look, I'm changing.

203

What do you call a T-Rex that's

been beaten up?

Dino-sore.

204

What did the axe murderer say to the judge?

It was an axe-ident.

How much does a Mustang cost?

More than you can af-Ford.

What do you call someone who plays

tricks on Halloween?

Prankenstein.

207

Why can't your nose be twelve inches long?

Because then it'd be
a foot.

208

Why did the pig get hired by the restaurant?

He was really good at bacon.

209

What do you call anxious dinosaurs?

Nervous Rex.

210

What do you call a snobbish criminal going down the stairs?

A condescending con descending.

211

Did you hear about the kidnapping at school?

He woke up.

212

I'M LIKE THE FABRIC VERSION OF KING MIDAS.

Everything I touch becomes felt.

213

My wife first agreed to a date after I gave her a bottle of tonic water.

I Schwepped her of her feet.

214

I always used to get small shocks when touching metal objects, but it recently stopped.

Needless to say, I'm ex-static.

215

Why do Norwegians build their own tables?

No Ikea!

216

WHY DID THE COFFEE GO TO THE POLICE?

It got mugged.

76

217

How many ears does Captain Kirk have?

Three: the left ear, the right ear, and the final frontier.

218

I knew I shouldn't have had the sea food.

I'm feeling a little eel.

219

What's made of brass and sounds like Tom Jones?

Trombones.

220

What do prisoners use to call each other?

Cell phones.

221

What do you call an old person with really good hearing?

Deaf-defying.

222

MY WIFE KEEPS TELLING ME TO STOP PRETENDING TO BE BUTTER.

But I'm on a roll now.

223

How does Darth Vader like his toast?

On the dark side.

224

I'm the Norse god of mischief, but I don't like to talk about it.

I guess you could say I'm low-key.

225

My wife says she's leaving me because she thinks I'm too obsessed with astronomy.

What planet is she on!

226

WHAT KIND OF TEA DO YOU DRINK WITH THE QUEEN?

Royal tea.

227

The circle is just the most ridiculous shape in the world.

There's absolutely no point to it.

228

There's been an explosion at a cheese factory in Paris.

There's nothing left but de Brie.

229

Last night, I had a dream that I was a muffler.

I woke up exhausted.

230

What are bald sea captains most worried about?

Cap sizes.

231

When is a cow hairy on the inside and the outside at the same time?

When it's stood in the doorway of the barn.

232

Where do you learn to make ice cream?

At sundae school.

233

Who was the roundest knight at King Arthur's round table?

Sir Cumference.

234

IF PRISONERS COULD TAKE THEIR OWN MUG SHOTS, WOULD THEY BE CALLED CELLFIES?

235

Why do chicken coops only have two doors?

Because if they had four doors,

they'd be chicken sedans.

236

DOGS CAN'T OPERATE MRI
MACHINES, BUT CATSCAN.

237

Did you hear about the restaurant on the

moon?

Great food, no atmosphere.

My son must have been relieved to have finally been born.

He looked like he was running out of womb in there.

What do you call a snowman with a six pack?

An abdominal snowman.

My mom bought me a really cheap dictionary for my birthday.

I couldn't find the words to thank her.

241

HOW MANY APPLES GROW ON A TREE?

All of them.

242

What do you call an explosive horse?

Neigh-palm.

243

I tried to have a conversation with my wife when she was applying a mud pack.

You should have seen the filthy look she gave me.

244

WHAT DO YOU CALL A HORSE THAT MOVES AROUND A LOT?

Unstable.

245

I just texted my girlfriend Ruth and told her

that it's over between us.

I'm Ruthless.

246

What type of magazines do cows read?

Cattlelogs.

247

WHAT DO YOU CALL A COW THAT JUST HAD A BABY?

DeCALFeinated or A New Moother

248

RIP BOILED WATER. YOU WILL BE MIST.

249

I DON'T TRUST STAIRS.

They're always up to something.

250

IF YOU WANT A JOB IN THE MOISTURIZER INDUSTRY, THE BEST ADVICE I CAN GIVE IS TO APPLY DAILY.

251

I hate perforated lines.

They're tearable.

252

WHEN MY WIFE TOLD ME TO STOP IMPERSONATING A FLAMINGO, I HAD TO PUT MY FOOT DOWN.

What do you call a can of soup that eats other cans of soup?

A CANnibal.

Why can't you hear a pterodactyl using the bathroom?

Because the P is silent.

THE ROTATION OF EARTH REALLY MAKES MY DAY.

256

Want to hear a joke about construction?

Nah, I'm still working on it.

257

You heard the rumor going around about butter?

Nevermind, I shouldn't spread it.

258

WHAT CONCERT COSTS ONLY 45 CENTS?

50 Cent ft. Nickelback.

259

What do they call Miley Cyrus in Europe?

Kilometry Cyrus.

260

I HAVE KLEPTOMANIA.

Sometimes when it gets really bad, I take something for it.

261

YOU SHOULDN'T KISS ANYONE ON JANUARY 1ST BECAUSE IT'S ONLY THE FIRST DATE.

262

If a child refuses to take a nap, is he resisting a rest?

263

What's the difference between a hippo and a zippo?

One is really heavy and the other is a little lighter.

264

WANT TO HEAR MY PIZZA JOKE?

Never mind, it's too cheesy.

265

What does a house wear?

A dress.

266

A furniture store keeps calling me.

But all I wanted was one night stand.

267

Why does Peter pan always fly?

Because he Neverlands!

My wife is on a tropical food diet; the house is full of the stuff.

It's enough to make a mango crazy.

MY WIFE TOLD ME I WAS AVERAGE, I THINK SHE'S MEAN.

270

HAD SEAFOOD LAST NIGHT, NOW I'M EEL.

I gave all my dead batteries away today . . .

Free of charge.

JUST QUIT MY JOB AT STARBUCKS BECAUSE DAY AFTER DAY IT WAS THE SAME OLD GRIND.

Went to the corner shop today . . .

Bought four corners.

274

How do you drown a hipster?

In the mainstream.

275

I'm thinking about getting a new haircut . . .

I'm going to mullet over.

276

Why couldn't the bicycle stand up by itself?

It was two tired.

277

WHAT DO YOU CALL SANTA'S HELPERS?

Subordinate clauses.

278

What time is it?

I don't know. It keeps changing.

279

A man knocked on my door and asked for a small donation for a local swimming pool.

So, I gave him a glass of water.

I went to a really emotional wedding

the other day . . .

Even the cake was in tiers.

I was getting into my car the other day and a man

asked: "Can you give me a lift?"

I said: "Sure, you look great, chase your dreams, go

for it!"

MY WIFE AND I WERE HAPPY FOR TWENTY YEARS.

But then we met.

How do prisoners call each other?

On their cell phones!

Did you hear about the man who lost his entire left side in an accident?

He's all right now.

285

Claustrophobic people are more productive

thinking outside the box.

286

PEOPLE WHO LACK THE PATIENCE FOR CALLIGRAPHY WILL NEVER HAVE PROPERLY FORMED CHARACTERS.

287

WAKING UP THIS MORNING WAS AN EYE-OPENING EXPERIENCE.

288

I tripped over my wife's bra.

It seemed to be a booby trap!

289

She had a photographic memory,

but never developed it.

290

MY MATH TEACHER CALLED ME AVERAGE. HOW MEAN!

SLEEPING COMES SO NATURALLY TO ME, I CAN DO IT WITH MY EYES CLOSED.

I had to quit my job at the shoe recycling factory.

It was just sole destroying.

Butchers link sausage to make ends meat.

294

Why didn't the lifeguard save the hippie?

Because he was too far out, man.

295

A train stops at a train station. A bus stops at a bus station.

Now, why is my desk called a "work station?"

296

I used to be a banker, but over time I lost interest.

The girl quit her job at the donut factory because she was fed up with the hole business.

I went to a buffet dinner with my neighbor, who is a taxidermist.

After such a big meal, I was stuffed.

A lawyer-turned-cook is a sue chef.

300

THE FOOD THEY SERVE TO GUARDS CAN LAST FOR SENTRIES.

301

HOW DO CONSTRUCTION WORKERS PARTY? THEY RAISE THE ROOF.

302

Tree trimmers do such a fantastic job, they should take a bough.

303

The librarian didn't know what to do with the book about Tesla's love of electricity, so he filed it under "Current Affairs."

304

After manually rotating the heavy machinery, the worker grew pretty cranky.

305

The inept psychic attempted clairvoyance, but just couldn't get intuit.

306

THE CARPENTER CAME 'ROUND THE OTHER DAY.

He made the best entrance I have ever seen . . .

307

TELLING A DEMOLITIONIST HOW TO DO HIS JOB IS DESTRUCTIVE CRITICISM.

308

Old artists never retire, they withdraw instead!

The key to job searching is looking deep within yourself.

It's all about the inner view.

THE OBSTETRICIANS SEEM TO CELEBRATE LABOR DAY EVERY SINGLE DAY!

The pilot was a loner but even for him flying a drone was simply too remote.

312

WHAT TYPE OF SHIRT DOES AN ASTRONAUT WEAR?

Apollo shirt.

313

I slept like a log during the night shift and I

was axed when I awoke!

314

The incompetent telegrapher was a weapon of

Morse destruction.

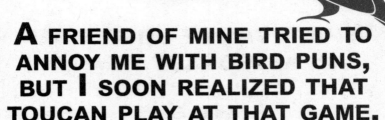

315

A FRIEND OF MINE TRIED TO ANNOY ME WITH BIRD PUNS, BUT I SOON REALIZED THAT TOUCAN PLAY AT THAT GAME.

316

The deer grabbed the gun and gave the hunter

a taste of his own venison.

317

Why did the bee get married?

Because he found his honey.

318

What did the buffalo say to his son when he left for college?

Bison.

319

WHY DO SEALS SWIM IN SALT WATER?

Because pepper water makes them sneeze.

320

PIG PUNS ARE REALLY BOARING.

321

A dog gave birth to puppies at the roadside and was fined for littering.

322

The best way to communicate with a fish is to drop them a line.

323

CUDDLING A CAT USUALLY LEAVES YOU FELINE GOOD.

What do you call a magic dog?

A Labracadabrador.

What do you call bees that are fat?

Obeese.

What do you call a cow eating grass?

A lawn-mooer.

What city has the largest rodent population?

Hamsterdam.

I'VE GOT A CHICKEN-PROOF GARDEN. IT'S COMPLETELY IMPECCABLE!

What do you call a cow with two legs?

Lean beef.

330

Which day do chickens hate the most?

Fry-day.

331

WHAT DO YOU CALL AN ALLIGATOR IN A VEST?

Investigator.

332

HAVE YOU EVER HEARD OF AN HONEST CHEETAH?

Why couldn't the chicken locate her eggs?

Because she had mislaid them.

What do you call a fish with no eyes?

A fsh.

WHY ARE MOST HORSES SO SLIM?

Because they are on a stable diet!

336

Why do cows wear bells?

Because their horns don't work!

337

What kind of pumpkin protects castles?

A royal gourd!

338

Even covered in salad dressing my lettuce looked bare, so I put some cloves on it.

339

Where do witches bake their cakes?

In a coven.

340

Two loaves of bread wanted to get married, which is why they eloafed.

341

I get distracted by all the meats in the deli section, must be my short attention spam.

342

WHAT ARE TWINS' FAVORITE FRUIT?

Pears!

343

Did you hear the joke about the peanut butter?

I'm not telling you. You might spread it!

344

Who's the king of vegetables?

Elvis Parsley.

345

WHY DID THE STUDENTS EAT THEIR HOMEWORK?

Their teacher said it was a piece of cake.

346

What do you call an almond in space?

An astronut.

347

WHY DIDN'T THE BANANA GO TO WORK?

It wasn't peeling well.

348

Why doesn't bread like warm weather?

Because it makes things toasty!

349

I always believed my body was a prison.

I was right, in biology, I learned it was made of cells.

350

The skeleton comic was trying tibia little humerus.

351

MASKS HAVE NO FACE VALUE!

352

Does my brand-new smile denture ego?

353

MY FRIEND STARTED TELLING ME SKELETON PUNS.

They were all extremely rib-tickling.

354

How do you capture a skeleton?

Use a rib-cage.

355

I'm friends with my fist, even though he's quite

a knuckle head.

356

THE CARDIOVASCULAR SYSTEM IS A WORK OF ARTERY, BUT IT IS ALSO PRETTY VEIN.

357

What did the bra say to the hat?

You go on a head while I give these two a lift.

358

Never date a tennis player.

Love means nothing to them.

359

I wondered why the baseball was getting bigger.

Then it hit me.

360

Why don't some couples go to the gym?

Because some relationships don't work out.

361

Do beginner vampires go to batting practice?

362

SINCE I QUIT SOCCER, I'VE LOST MY LIFE GOALS.

363

I lift weights only on Saturday and Sunday because Monday to Friday are weak days.

364

I'M NOT A HUGE FAN OF ARCHERY.

It has way too many drawbacks!

365

My snowboarding skills are really going downhill fast!

My tennis opponent was not happy with my service.

He kept returning it.

I quit gymnastics because I was fed up of hanging around the bars.

A FISHERMAN TRIED BOXING, BUT HE ONLY THREW HOOKS.

What should you say to impatient jockeys?

Hold your horses.

The race car driver had a pretty checkered past. . . .

Old skiers go downhill fast. . . .

372

THE WEIGH-IN AT THE SUMO WRESTLING CHAMPIONSHIP WAS A LARGE SCALE EFFORT.

373

Why was the referee fired?

Because he was a whistle blower!

374

After a long time waiting for the bowling alley to open, we eventually got the ball rolling.

375

I COULDN'T QUITE REMEMBER HOW TO THROW A BOOMERANG, BUT EVENTUALLY, IT CAME BACK TO ME.

376

Refusing to go to the gym counts as resistance training, right?

377

I'm taking part in a stair-climbing competition.

Guess I better step up my game.

378

Why do soccer players do so well in math?

They know how to use their heads!

379

Why was Cinderella banned from playing sports?

Because she always ran away from the ball.

380

I can't understand why people are so bothered about me not knowing what the word "apocalypse" means.

It's not like it's the end of the world!

381

I WAS THINKING ABOUT GETTING A BRAIN TRANSPLANT, BUT THEN I CHANGED MY MIND.

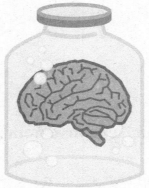

382

To the guy who invented zero:

Thanks for nothing!

383

WHERE DO BABY SPOONS COME FROM?

The spork delivers them.

384

The man's zipper broke, but he fixed it

on the fly.

385

A hair-raising experience sounds promising to

a bald man.

386

It was cold in the bedroom, so I laid down in the fireplace and slept like a log.

387

DON'T SPELL "PART" BACKWARDS.

It's a trap!

388

Why don't cannibals eat clowns?

They taste rather funny.

389

I recently got crushed by a pile of books, but I suppose I've only got my shelf to blame.

390

I've decided to sell my vacuum.

Well, it was just gathering dust!

391

I saw a documentary on how ships are kept together.

Riveting!

392

I've been reading a book about anti-gravity.

It's impossible to put down.

393

HAVE YOU HEARD ABOUT THE MAGIC TRACTOR?

It turned into a field!

394

I couldn't work out how to fasten my seatbelt for ages.

But then one day, it just clicked.

395

Yesterday, I accidentally swallowed some food coloring.

The doctor says I'm OK, but I feel like I've dyed a little inside.

396

I'd tell you a chemistry joke, but I know I wouldn't get a reaction.

397

Have you ever tried to eat a clock?

It's very time-consuming.

398

I didn't use to like duct-tape at first,

but I soon became attached to it.

399

The newspaper's rationale for running the

story was paper thin.

400

I really wanted a camouflage cap,

but I couldn't find one.

401

I planned to find my watch today, but I didn't

have the time.

402

WHERE DID NOAH KEEP HIS BEES?

In the ark hives.

403

DID YOU HEAR ABOUT THE RESTAURANT ON THE MOON?

Great food; no atmosphere.

404

WHAT DO YOU CALL A FAKE NOODLE?

An impasta.

405

How many apples grow on a tree?

All of them.

406

Want to hear a joke about paper?

Never mind, it's tearable.

407

I just watched a program about beavers.

It was the best dam program I've ever seen.

408

What's the difference between a well-dressed man on a bicycle and a poorly dressed man on a unicycle?

Attire.

How does a penguin build its house?

Igloos it together.

SON: Dad, did you get a haircut?
DAD: No, I got them all cut.

What do you call a Mexican

who has lost his car?

Carlos.

Son: Dad, can you put my shoes on?

Dad: No, I don't think they'll fit me.

Why did the scarecrow win an award?

Because he was outstanding in his field.

WHY DON'T SKELETONS EVER GO TRICK OR TREATING?

Because they have no body to go with.

Daughter: I'll call you later.

Dad: Don't call me later, call me Dad.

What do you call an elephant that doesn't matter?

An irrelephant.

Want to hear a joke about construction?

I'm still working on it.

418

What do you call cheese that isn't yours?

Nacho Cheese.

419

WHY COULDN'T THE BICYCLE STAND UP BY ITSELF?

It was two tired.

420

What did the grape do when

he got stepped on?

He let out a little wine.

I wouldn't buy anything with velcro.

It's a total rip-off.

THE SHOVEL WAS A GROUND-BREAKING INVENTION.

Daughter: Dad, can you put the cat out?

Dad: I didn't know it was on fire!

424

This graveyard looks overcrowded. . . .

People must be dying to get in there.

425

Cashier: Would you like your milk in a bag?

Dad: No, just leave it in the carton!

426

5/4 OF PEOPLE ADMIT THAT THEY'RE BAD WITH FRACTIONS.

Two goldfish are in a tank.

One says to the other, "Do you know

how to drive this thing?"

WHAT DO YOU CALL A MAN WITH A RUBBER TOE?

Roberto.

What do you call a fat psychic?

A four-chin teller.

430

I would avoid the sushi if I were you.

It's a little fishy.

431

To the man in the wheelchair who stole my camouflage jacket . . . you can hide, but you can't run.

432

THE ROTATION OF EARTH REALLY MAKES MY DAY.

433

I thought about going on an all-almond diet.

But that's just nuts.

434

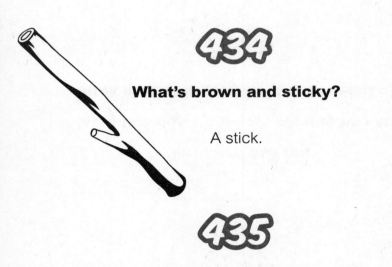

What's brown and sticky?

A stick.

435

I've never gone to a gun range before.

I decided to give it a shot!

436

Why do you never see elephants

hiding in trees?

Because they're so good at it.

437

Did you hear about the kidnapping at school?

It's fine, he woke up.

438

A FURNITURE STORE KEEPS CALLING ME.

All I wanted was
one night stand.

439

I used to work in a shoe recycling shop.

It was sole destroying.

440

Did I tell you the time I fell in

love during a backflip?

I was heels over head.

441

I don't play soccer because I enjoy the

sport. . . .

I'm just doing it for kicks.

442

PEOPLE DON'T LIKE HAVING TO BEND OVER TO GET THEIR DRINKS.

We really need to raise the bar.

443

Were you there when the TV repairman got married?

The reception was excellent.

444

DID YOU HEAR ABOUT THE DENTIST AND THE MANICURIST?

They fought tooth and nail.

445

My doctor told me I had type A blood. . . .

But it was a Type-O.

446

Why were the Indians here first?

They had reservations.

447

If a seagull flies over the sea, what flies over the bay?

A bagel.

448

What do you call a veterinarian with laryngitis?

A hoarse doctor.

449

DID YOU HEAR ABOUT THE CANNIBAL WHO WAS LATE FOR DINNER?

He got the cold shoulder.

450

How did Hitler tie his laces?

In little Nazis.

451

Why do ambassadors never get sick?

Diplomatic immunity.

452

What happens to deposed kings?

They get throne away.

453

What kind of tree do fingers grow on?

A palm tree.

454

WHAT DO YOU CALL A BABY MONKEY?

A chimp off the old block.

455

What has four wheels and flies?

A garbage truck.

WHAT DOES A SPY DO WHEN HE GETS COLD?

He goes undercover.

What did the alien dandelion say

to the Earth dandelion?

"Take me to your weeder!"

Why does lightning shock people?

Because it doesn't know how to conduct itself.

459

Why did the little boy sleep on the chandelier?

Because he was a light sleeper.

460

What do prisoners use to call each other?

Cell phones.

461

How do you tickle a rich girl?

Say, "Gucci, Gucci, Gucci!"

462

Where did the king put his armies?

In his sleevies.

463

WHY DON'T CANNIBALS EAT CLOWNS?

Because they taste funny.

464

What is copper nitrate?

Overtime for policemen.

465

How do crazy people go through the forest?

They take the psycho-path.

466

WHAT DID THE COACH SAY TO HIS LOSING TEAM OF SNAKES?

"You can't venom all."

467

How do you change tires on a duck?

With a quackerjack.

468

What is a mouse's favorite game?

Hide and Squeak.

469

What do you call a train loaded with toffee?

A chew chew train.

470

When does a boat show affection?

When it hugs the shore.

471

WHAT DO YOU CALL A FISH WITH NO EYES?

A fsh.

472

Which president

was least guilty?

Lincoln. He's in a cent.

473

What do you call a rabbit with fleas?

Bugs Bunny.

WHAT IS THE PURPOSE OF REINDEER?

It makes the grass grow, sweetie.

What did the guitar say to the musician?

"Pick on someone your own size!"

What do you call Santa's helpers?

Subordinate Clauses.

477

WHAT DO YOU CALL TWO PEOPLE IN AN AMBULANCE?

A pair of medics.

478

Why are rivers always rich?

Because they have two banks.

479

What's the best time to go to the dentist?

Tooth hurty.

What must you know to be an auctioneer?

Lots.

What do you call a cow who gives no milk?

A milk dud.

WHAT DID THE TOY STORE SIGN SAY?

"Don't feed the animals. They are already stuffed."

Did you hear about the dyslexic Satanist?

He sold his soul to Santa.

484

What do you get when you drop a piano down a mineshaft?

A flat miner.

485

Why aren't Greeks morning people?

Because Dawn is tough on grease.

How can a leopard change his spots?

By moving.

Why are meteorologists always nervous?

Their future is always up in the air.

What do you call a dinosaur

with an extensive vocabulary?

A thesaurus.

489

What is the difference between

one yard and two yards?

A fence.

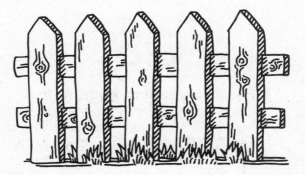

490

I DIDN'T LIKE MY BEARD AT FIRST. . . .

Then it grew on me.

491

What do you get from a pampered cow?

Spoiled milk.

492

Where do you find giant nails?

On the ends of giants' fingers.

493

What's a three-season bed?

One without a spring.

Why do cows wear cowbells?

Because their horns don't work.

WHAT DISNEY MOVIE IS ABOUT A STUPID BOYFRIEND?

Dumb Beau.

496

WHAT MUSICAL IS ABOUT A TRAIN CONDUCTOR?

"My Fare, Lady"

497

I'm like the fabric version of King Midas. . . .

Everything I touch becomes felt.

498

My wife first agreed to a date after I gave her a bottle of tonic water.

I Schwepped her off her feet.

499

I always used to get small shocks when touching metal objects, but it recently stopped.

Needless to say, I'm ex-static.

500

Why do Norwegians build their own tables?

No Ikea!

501

Why did the coffee go to the police?

It got mugged.

502

HOW MANY EARS DOES CAPTAIN KIRK HAVE?

Three: the left ear, the right ear, and the final frontier.

503

I knew I shouldn't have had the seafood.

I'm feeling a little eel.

504

**What's made of brass and
sounds like Tom Jones?**

Trombones.

505

**What do you call an old person with really
good hearing?**

Deaf defying.

506

**MY WIFE KEEPS TELLING
ME TO STOP PRETENDING
TO BE BUTTER.**

But I'm on a roll now.

507

Why can't you be friends with a chipmunk?

They drive everyone nuts!

508

I tried drag racing the other day.

It's murder trying to

run in heels.

HOW DOES DARTH VADER LIKE HIS TOAST?

On the dark side.

A proud new dad sits down with his own father for a celebratory drink.

His father says, "Son, now you've got a child of your own, I think it's time you had this."

And with that, he pulls out a book called, "1001 Dad Jokes".

The new dad says, "Dad, I'm honored," as tears well up in his eyes.

His father says, "Hi Honored, I'm Dad."

511

What kind of tea do you drink with the Queen?

Royal tea.

512

My wife says she's leaving me because she thinks I'm too obsessed with astronomy.

What planet is she on!?

513

I'm the Norse god of mischief but I don't like to talk about it.

I guess you could say I'm low-key.

What do you call a woman who

sounds like an ambulance?

Nina.

THE CIRCLE IS JUST THE MOST RIDICULOUS SHAPE IN THE WORLD.

There's absolutely no point to it.

516

There's been an explosion at a cheese factory in Paris.

There's nothing left but de brie.

517

Last night, I had a dream that I was a muffler . . .

I woke up exhausted.

518

WHAT ARE BALD SEA CAPTAINS MOST WORRIED ABOUT?

Cap sizes.

519

No matter how kind you are . . .

German children are kinder.

520

When is a cow hairy on the inside and the outside at the same time?

When it's standing in the doorway of the barn.

521

WHAT DO YOU CALL A SNOWMAN WITH A SIX PACK?

An abdominal snowman.

522

**After dinner, my wife asked me
if I could clear the table.**

I needed a run-up, but I made it.

523

**Who was the roundest knight at King Arthur's
round table?**

Sir Cumference.

524

As I handed my Dad his 50th birthday card, he looked at me with tears in his eyes and said . . .

"You know, one would have been enough."

525

If prisoners could take their own mug shots, would they be called cellfies?

526

Why do chicken coops only have two doors?

Because if they had four doors, they'd be chicken sedans.

527

Where do you learn to make ice cream?

At sundae school.

528

DOGS CAN'T OPERATE MRI MACHINES . . .

But catscan.

I got an e-mail saying, "At Google Earth, we can read maps backwards!" and I thought . . .

"That's just spam."

I can't stand stair lifts.

They drive me up the wall!

How do you tell the difference between a frog and a horny toad?

A frog says, "Ribbit, Ribbit" and a horny toad says, "Rub it, Rub it".

532

My son must have been relieved

to have finally been born. . . .

He looked like he was running out of womb in there.

533

WHAT HAS TWO BUTTS AND KILLS PEOPLE?

An assassin.

534

What do you call a cake baked by a hooker?

Hoe-made.

My mom bought me a really cheap dictionary

for my birthday.

I couldn't find the words to thank her.

My friend and I started a new band and

decided to call ourselves "Duvet" . . .

We only do covers.

WHAT DO YOU CALL AN EXPLOSIVE HORSE?

Neigh-palm.

538

**What type of
magazines do cows read?**

Cattlelogs.

539

**I tried to have a conversation with my wife
when she was applying a mud pack.**

You should have seen the filthy look she gave me.

540

**A Dutchman has invented shoes that record
how many miles you've walked.**

Clever clogs.

What do you call a horse that moves around a lot?

Unstable.

I JUST TEXTED MY GIRLFRIEND RUTH AND TOLD HER THAT IT'S OVER BETWEEN US.

I'm Ruthless.

One of the Russian acrobats in our human

pyramid has been deported.

We don't have Oleg to stand on.

Why can't a nose be 12 inches long?

Because then it'd be a foot.

Why does Piglet smell?

Because he plays with Pooh.

Why did Mozart kill all his chickens?

Because when he asked them who the best composer was, they all said, "Bach, Bach, Bach."

547

What is a ninja's favorite type of shoe?

Sneakers.

548

Why do crabs never give to charity?

Because they're shellfish.

549

How do astronomers organize a party?

They planet.

550

**How do you know when you're
going to drown in milk?**

When it's past your eyes.

551

**WHEN YOU HAVE A BLADDER
INFECTION, URINE TROUBLE.**

552

**OUR WEDDING WAS SO
BEAUTIFUL . . .**

even the cake was in tiers.

553

What did one plate say to the other?

"Lunch is on me!"

554

Did you hear about the guy

who invented Lifesavers?

They say he made a mint.

555

How do you make anti-freeze?

Take away her blanket.

556

WHAT DID THE BIG CHIMNEY SAY TO THE LITTLE CHIMNEY?

"You're too young to be smoking."

557

What's the difference between bird flu and swine flu?

If you have bird flu, you need tweet-ment. If you have swine flu, you need oink-ment.

558

Why don't dinosaurs talk?

Because they're dead.

What does a martial arts expert drink?

Kara-tea.

How do fish get high?

Seaweed.

Why did Humpty Dumpty have a great fall?

To make up for an awful summer.

562

WHY DO GHOSTS LOVE ELEVATORS?

Because they lift their spirits.

563

What sound does a nut make when it sneezes?

"Cashew!"

564

What did the tie say to the neck?

"I think I'll just hang around."

565

What's a frog's favorite drink?

Croak-a Cola.

566

What's a dentist's favorite musical instrument?

A tuba toothpaste.

567

DID YOU HEAR ABOUT THAT NEW MOVIE CALLED CONSTIPATION?

No? That's because it's not out yet.

568

What do you call a fly with no wings?

A walk.

569

What do you call the security guards outside the Samsung factory?

The Guardians of the Galaxy.

570

What do you call a horse who likes arts and crafts?

A hobby horse.

How did the hipster burn his mouth?

He drank his coffee before it was cool.

Who writes ghost stories?

A ghost writer.

573

How do you catch a bra?

With a booby trap.

574

HOW MANY LIVES DOES A GERMAN CAT HAVE?

Nein.

575

What do you call a crab that plays baseball?

A pinch hitter.

576

A devout Christian guy went to a remote island to work as a missionary but was captured by a tribe of cannibals who cooked and ate him.

He was very tender and tasty, but they were all violently sick afterwards.

It just goes to show that you can't keep a good man down.

577

A hungry traveler stopped at a monastery and was taken to the kitchens where a brother is frying chips.

"Are you the friar?" he asked.

The brother replied, "No. I'm the chip monk."

A DOCTOR HAD A REGULAR HABIT OF STOPPING OFF AT A BAR FOR A HAZELNUT DAIQUIRI ON HIS WAY HOME EVERY EVENING. THE BARTENDER LEARNED HIS HABIT AND WOULD ALWAYS HAVE THE DRINK WAITING AT PRECISELY 5:03 P.M.

ONE AFTERNOON, AS FIVE O'CLOCK APPROACHED, THE BARTENDER WAS DISMAYED TO FIND THAT HE WAS OUT OF HAZELNUT EXTRACT.

THINKING QUICKLY, HE THREW TOGETHER A DAIQUIRI MADE WITH HICKORY NUTS AND SET IT ON THE BAR.

THE DOCTOR CAME IN AT HIS REGULAR TIME, TOOK ONE SIP OF THE DRINK, AND EXCLAIMED, "THIS ISN'T A HAZELNUT DAIQUIRI!"

"NO, I'M SORRY," REPLIED THE BARTENDER, "IT'S A HICKORY DAIQUIRI, DOC."

579

A guy goes to a psychiatrist and says, "Doc, I keep having these alternating, recurring dreams. First, I'm a teepee; then I'm a wigwam; then I'm a teepee; then I'm a wigwam. It's driving me crazy. What's wrong with me?"

The doctor replies, "It's very simple. You're two tents."

580

Two boll weevils grew up in South Carolina. One went to Hollywood and, amazingly, became a famous actor. The other stayed behind in the cotton fields and never amounted to much.

The second one, naturally, became known as the lesser of two weevils.

581

DID YOU HEAR ABOUT THE BUDDHIST WHO REFUSED NOVOCAIN DURING A ROOT CANAL?

He wanted to transcend dental medication.

582

Mahatma Gandhi, as everyone knows, walked barefoot most of the time, which produced an impressive set of calluses on his feet.

He also ate very little, which made him rather frail, and with his odd diet he suffered from bad breath.

This made him a super-calloused fragile mystic hexed by halitosis.

583

A boy had a job bagging groceries at a supermarket. One day, the store installed a machine for squeezing fresh orange juice.

Intrigued, the young man eventually asked if he could be allowed to work the machine, but the store manager turned down his request, saying, "Sorry, kid, but baggers can't be juicers."

584

What do a law student and a recovering alcoholic have in common?

They both have to pass the bar.

585

Two Eskimos sitting in a kayak were chilly, so they lit a fire in the craft.

Unsurprisingly, it sank, proving once again that you can't have your kayak and heat it too.

586

PEOPLE ARE USUALLY SHOCKED WHEN THEY FIND OUT I'M NOT A VERY GOOD ELECTRICIAN.

587

Why do bears have heavy coats?

Fur protection.

A SNAKE WALKS INTO A BAR.

The bartender asks, "How'd you do that?!"

Marriage is grand.

Divorce is a hundred grand.

My wife gave birth in the car

on the way to the hospital.

She named him Carson.

591

WHY CAN'T A MAN STARVE IN THE DESERT?

Because of all the
sand which is there.

592

I accidentally swallowed a bunch of Scrabble tiles.

My next trip to the bathroom could spell disaster.

593

I have a steering

wheel on my crotch.

It's driving me nuts.

594

To whoever stole my antidepressants,

I hope you're happy.

595

You can never run through campgrounds.

You can only ran, because it's past tents.

596

What would you get if you stacked all the

terrible dad jokes in a circle?

Groanhenge.

AT WHAT TEMPERATURE DO THEY KEEP BLANKETS FOR NEWBORNS?

Womb temperature.

Children in the dark make accidents.

But accidents in the dark make children.

599

Someone sent me a video on WhatsApp saying, "I bet you can't watch this for more than 10 seconds!"

He was absolutely right . . . the video was only 5 seconds long.

600

I HAVE A GOOD JOKE ABOUT TIME TRAVEL, BUT YOU DIDN'T LIKE IT.

601

Two knights were fighting when one of them got their feet chopped off.

He was defeated.

602

There's a really talented magician who speaks Spanish.

He goes to a party and says, "Alright, I'm going to disappear on the count of three: uno . . . dos . . ."

. . . and he was gone without a tres.

603

I'm not addicted to brake fluid . . .

I can stop whenever I want.

604

I HEARD A LITTLE PUN THE OTHER DAY.

It wasn't fully groan.

605

Why did the "A" go into the bathroom and come out an "E"?

He had a vowel movement.

606

Why does Snoop Dogg carry an umbrella?

Fo' drizzle!

607

Why don't dolphins ever make mistakes?

Everything they do is on porpoise!

608

A COW WALKS INTO A POT FIELD.

The steaks have never been higher.

609

I'm sad I didn't get to see

how my execution ended. . . .

I was left hanging.

610

Apparently, you can't use "beefstew"

as a password.

It's not stroganoff.

611

I thought swimming with the dolphins was

expensive . . .

but swimming with the sharks cost me an arm and a leg!

612

I BLINDFOLDED MY WIFE
WITH A SCARF YESTERDAY.

I really pulled the wool
over her eyes.

613

I used to wonder where the

sun went at night. . . .

Then it dawned on me.

614

My wife burned her tongue drinking

scalding hot coffee, and I thought of

making a joke about it.

But then realized it would be in poor taste.

615

I asked my daughter if she'd seen my newspaper. She told me that newspapers are old school. She said that people use tablets nowadays and handed me her iPad.

The fly didn't stand a chance. . . .

616

Rumor has it that Uranus has a black hole in the center of it.

SOME GERMAN CARS ARE VERY QUIET.

They are barely audi-ble.

I don't like jokes about canned meat.

They're mostly spam.

Have you heard of the new hipster weather

forecasting device?

It lets you know when temperatures are dropping

before anyone thinks they're cool.

620

Want to hear a pizza joke?

Never mind, it's too cheesy.

621

What do you call a fish with no legs?

A fish.

622

A SHIPMENT OF VIAGRA HAS BEEN STOLEN

Police looking for hardened criminals.

623

You know the problem with grapes these days?

People just aren't raisin them right.

624

SINGING IN THE SHOWER IS ALL FUN AND GAMES, UNTIL YOU GET SOAP IN YOUR MOUTH. . . .

Then it becomes a soap opera.

625

What do you call a diced potato?

A squared root.

626

How do you know a wishing well works?

If your mother-in-law falls down it.

627

WHAT ROOMS DO GHOSTS AVOID?

Living rooms.

628

Man 1: Why did you buy a camouflage toilet seat?

Man 2: So my wife can't yell at me when I miss!

What did the elephant say to the naked man?

"How do you breathe through that tiny trunk?"

An amnesiac walks into a bar, goes up to a beautiful blonde, and says, "So, do I come here often?"

Patient: "I was thinking about getting a vasectomy."

Doctor: "That's a big decision. Have you talked it over with your family?"

Patient: "Yes, we took a vote and they're in favor of it 17 to 2."

632

A woman sees her husband standing on the bathroom scale, sucking in his stomach. "You know that's not going to help, right?" she asks.

"Sure it will," he says. "It's the only way I'll be able to see the numbers."

633

SON: Dad, do you know the difference between a pack of cookies and a pack of elephants?
DAD: No.
SON: Then it's a good thing Mom does the grocery shopping!

634

Son: Daddy, can I have a glass of water please?

Dad: I've given you six glasses of water already!

Son: Yes, but the backyard is still on fire!

635

Why do dads take an extra pair of socks when they go golfing on Father's Day?

In case they get a hole in one!

636

Dad: Son, if you keep pulling my hair, you will have to get off my shoulders.

Son: But, Dad, I'm just trying to get my gum back!

Son: For $20, I'll be good.

Dad: Oh, yeah? When I was your age,

I was good for nothing.

WHAT DID THE FISH SAY WHEN HE HIT A CONCRETE WALL?

"Dam."

A married couple was in a terrible accident where

the woman's face was severely burned. The doctor

told the husband that they couldn't graft any skin

from her body because she was too skinny. So, the husband offered to donate some of his own skin. However, the only skin on his body that the doctor felt was suitable would have to come from his buttocks.

The husband and wife agreed that they would tell no one about where the skin came from and requested that the doctor also honor their secret. After all, this was a very delicate matter.

After the surgery was completed, everyone was astounded at the woman's new beauty. She looked more beautiful than she ever had before! All her friends and relatives just went on and on about her youthful beauty!

One day, she was alone with her husband, and she was overcome with emotion at his sacrifice. She said, "Dear, I just want to thank you for everything you did for me. There is no way I could ever repay you."

"My darling," he replied, "think nothing of it. I get all the thanks I need every time I see your mother kiss you on the cheek."

WHAT DO ESKIMOS GET FROM SITTING ON THE ICE TOO LONG?

Polaroids.

HOW DO YOU GET HOLY WATER?

Boil the hell out of it.

What do the letters D.N.A. stand for?

National Dyslexic Association.

What do you get when you cross a snowman

with a vampire?

Frostbite.

What has four legs, is big, green, and fuzzy,

and if it fell out of a tree would kill you?

A pool table.

Why are there so many Smiths in the phone book?

They all have phones.

WHAT DO YOU CALL A HIPPIE'S WIFE?

Mississippi.

What do you get when you cross

a pit bull with a collie?

A dog that runs for help after it bites your leg off.

648

What does it mean when the flag is at half-mast at the post office?

They're hiring.

649

I DREAMED I WAS DROWNING IN AN OCEAN OF ORANGE SODA LAST NIGHT.

It took me a while to work out that it was just a Fanta sea.

650

At work we have a printer that we named Bob Marley.

It's always jammin'.

651

I've decided Hershey's chocolate is too feminist for my taste.

I'm switching to Hishey's.

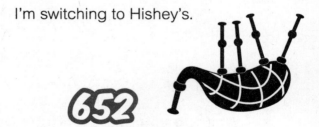

652

Why do bagpipers walk when they play?

They're trying to get away from the noise.

I start a new job in Seoul next week.

I hope it's going to be a good Korea move.

DO I ENJOY MAKING COURTHOUSE PUNS?

Guilty.

What do you call a sketchy Italian

neighborhood?

The spaghetto.

656

I got caught stealing a leg of lamb

from the supermarket.

The security guard said, "What do you

think you're doing with that?"

I replied, "Potatoes, peas, and gravy

would be nice."

657

I CAN'T DECIDE IF I WANT TO PURSUE A CAREER AS A WRITER OR A GRIFTER.

I'm still weighing the prose and cons.

I don't often tell dad jokes,

but when I do, he laughs.

A man walks into a bookstore and asks,

"Can I have a book by Shakespeare?"

"Of course, sir, which one?"

"William."

660

Accordion to a recent survey, inserting

musical instruments into sentences

largely goes unnoticed.

I don't know why Marvel hasn't tried to put advertisements on the Hulk.

He's essentially a giant Banner.

I'll never date another apostrophe.

The last one was too possessive.

WHAT DO YOU CALL A ROW OF PEOPLE LIFTING MOZZARELLA?

A cheesy pick up line.

What's Donald Trump's favorite brand of gum?

Bigly chew.

WHY CAN'T YOU EAT WOOKIE MEAT?

Because it's too Chewy.

People tell me the story of Jesus is made up. . . .

But I think it Israel.

A grasshopper walks into a bar.

The bartender says, "I'm going to serve you a drink named after you."

The grasshopper replies, "You have a drink named Steve?!"

I gave all my dead batteries away,

free of charge.

669

What would *Rocky* be called

if it was a hockey movie?

Rockey.

670

I dig, you dig, we dig, she digs, he digs, they dig.

It's not a beautiful poem, but it's very deep.

671

Dad: "You know how scuba divers sit on the edge of the boat and fall out backwards into the water? You know why they do that?"

Son: "No, why?"

Dad: "If they went forward they'd fall into the boat!"

672

IT'S REALLY HARD TO SAY WHAT MY WIFE DOES FOR A LIVING.

She sells sea shells by the sea shore.

673

I just swapped our bed for a trampoline.

My wife hit the roof.

674

My wife is really mad at the fact

that I have no sense of direction.

So I packed up my stuff and right.

675

TODAY, MY SON ASKED, "CAN I HAVE A BOOKMARK?" AND I BURST INTO TEARS. . . .

11 years old and he still doesn't know my name is Brian.

676

DAD: I was just listening to the radio on my way into town. Apparently an actress just killed herself.

MOM: Oh my! Who!?

DAD: Uh, I can't remember. . . . I think her name was Reese something?

MOM: WITHERSPOON?!

DAD: No, it was with a knife. . . .

677

I bought some shoes from a drug dealer.

I don't know what he laced them with, but I was tripping all day!

678

Did you know the first french fries weren't actually cooked in France?

They were cooked in Greece.

679

IF A CHILD REFUSES TO SLEEP DURING NAP TIME, ARE THEY GUILTY OF RESISTING A REST?

680

The secret service isn't allowed to yell "Get down!" anymore when the president is about to be attacked.

Now they have to yell, "Donald, duck!"

681

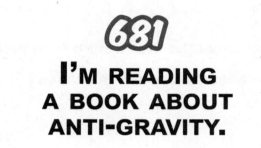

I'M READING A BOOK ABOUT ANTI-GRAVITY.

It's impossible to put down!

682

What do you call someone with no body and no nose?

Nobody knows.

683

A slice of apple pie is $2.50 in Jamaica and $3.00 in the Bahamas.

These are the pie rates of the Caribbean.

684

What is the least spoken language in the world?

Sign language.

685

My daughter screeched, "Daaaaaad, you haven't listened to one word I've said, have you!?"

What a strange way to start a conversation with me. . . .

686

I ORDERED A CHICKEN AND AN EGG FROM AMAZON . . . I'LL LET YOU KNOW.

687

My wife tried to unlatch our daughter's car seat with one hand and asked, "How do one-armed mothers do it?"

Without missing a beat, I replied, "Single handedly."

688

My friend keeps saying "Cheer up, man, it could be worse. You could be stuck underground in a hole full of water."

I know he means well.

689

Justice is a dish best served cold.

If it were served warm it would be justwater.

690

MOM: "How do I look?"

DAD: "With your eyes."

691

**Spring is here! I got so
excited I wet my plants!**

692

3 UNWRITTEN RULES OF LIFE:

1.
2.
3.

693

IF YOU SEE A ROBBERY AT AN APPLE STORE DOES THAT MAKE YOU AN iWITNESS?

694

Did you hear that FedEx and UPS are merging?

They're going to go by the name Fed-Up from now on.

695

KID: "Dad, make me a sandwich!"

DAD: "Poof, you're a sandwich!"

I told my son I was named after

Thomas Jefferson . . . He said,

"But Dad, your name is Brian."

I said, "I know, but I was named AFTER

Thomas Jefferson."

Don't trust atoms.

They make up everything!

Why did the invisible man turn down the job offer?

He couldn't see himself doing it.

SERVER: "Sorry about your wait."

DAD: "Are you saying I'm fat?"

WHAT'S THE BEST PART ABOUT LIVING IN SWITZERLAND?

I don't know, but the flag is a big plus.

701

If Snoop Dogg dies before pot becomes legal

in the US, he will be rolling in his grave.

702

WHAT DO YOU CALL A DOG THAT CAN DO MAGIC?

A Labracadabrador.

703

What do you call a deer with no eyes?

No idea!

704

GRANDPA: I have a "dad bod."

DAD: To me it's more like a father figure.

705

WHAT'S FORREST GUMP'S PASSWORD?

1forrest1.

706

I used to have a job at a calendar factory . . .

but I got the sack because I took a couple of days off.

707

Why didn't the vampire attack Taylor Swift?

She had bad blood.

708

Why did Santa go to college for music?

So he could improve his wrapping skills.

709

I asked the lion in the wardrobe

what he was doing there . . .

He said it was Narnia business!

710

Did you hear about the dog who gave

birth on the side of the road?

She was ticketed for littering.

711

A SHEEP, A DRUM, AND A SNAKE FALL OVER A CLIFF . . .

Ba-Dum-Tss.

712

Man: Waiter, this coffee tastes like mud!

Waiter: Yes sir, it is fresh ground.

713

I used to be a banker . . .

But then I lost interest.

714

WHY DID ADELE CROSS THE ROAD?

To say hello from the other side.

715

I should have been sad when my flashlight batteries died. . . .

But I was delighted.

716

Why isn't Cinderella good at soccer?

Because her coach is a pumpkin and she keeps running away from the ball!

717

SOMEONE THREW A BOTTLE OF OMEGA-3 PILLS AT ME.

Luckily, my injuries were only super fish oil.

718

A guitarist passed out on stage.

He must have rocked himself to sleep.

719

Did you hear about

the important pickle?

It was a big dill!

256

Why can't you give Elsa a balloon?

Because she'll let it go.

Why don't you iron a four-leaf clover?

Because you don't want to press your luck.

How much room is needed for fungi to grow?

As mushroom as possible!

723

WHY DOES WALDO ALWAYS WEAR STRIPES?

Because he doesn't want to be spotted.

724

Tried to catch fog yesterday. . . .

Mist.

725

I have a lot of jokes about

unemployed people . . .

but none of them work.

726

WHEN CHEMISTS DIE, THEY BARIUM.

727

Jokes about German sausage are the würst.

728

I took a class trip to the

Coca-Cola Museum.

I hope there's no pop quiz.

How does Moses make his tea?

Hebrews it.

This girl said she recognized me from the vegetarian club, but I'd never met herbivore.

I did a theatrical performance about puns.

It was a play on words.

PMS JOKES AREN'T FUNNY, PERIOD.

What do you call a soldier who survived

mustard gas and pepper spray?

A seasoned veteran.

ENERGIZER BUNNY ARRESTED. CHARGED WITH BATTERY.

Did you hear the joke about the dry erase board?

It's remarkable!

I got a job at a bakery because

I kneaded the dough.

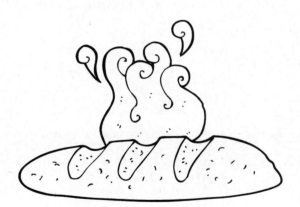

737

England has no kidney bank,

but it does have a Liverpool.

738

I dropped out of Communism class

because of lousy Marx.

739

All the toilets in New York City's
police stations have been stolen.
Police have nothing to go on.

740

What does a clock do when it's hungry?

Go back four seconds.

741

**Haunted French pancakes
give me the crèpes.**

742

**I wondered why the baseball
was getting bigger. . . .**

Then it hit me!

743

Cartoonist found dead in home.
Details are sketchy.

744

Venison for dinner?

Oh deer!

745

**I USED TO THINK I WAS
INDECISIVE, BUT NOW I'M
NOT SO SURE. . . .**

746

Be kind to your dentist.

He has fillings too.

747

What do you call a potato wearing sunglasses?

A spectater.

748

Dad: There's going to be thousands of people in Bristol tonight.

Son: Why?

Dad: Because they live there!

749

HOW DOES THE MAN ON THE MOON GET HIS HAIR CUT?

Eclipse it.

750

Brother: What would you do if I fell down a cliff?

Sister: I'd call you an ambulance, of course!

Dad: How would that help? He's at the bottom

of a cliff dying, and you're shouting, "YOU'RE AN

AMBULANCE!"

How do you hide an elephant?

You paint it red! Have you ever seen

a red elephant? I didn't think so!

Dad: What comes after S in the alphabet?

Daughter: T?

Dad: I'll have milk and two sugars, thanks!

753

Why isn't dark spelled with a "c" instead of a "k?"

Because you can't see in the dark!

754

WHY DOES ED SHEERAN NOT HAVE A GIRLFRIEND?

Because Sheeran away.

755

Two years ago, my doctor told me I was going deaf.

I haven't heard from him since.

756

**Remember when air for your tires
was free and now it's $1.50?**

It's because of inflation.

757

**What will a dad say if you
ask him if he's alright?**

"No, I'm half left."

758

Son: Hey, I was thinking . . .

Dad: I thought I smelled something burning!

759

TWO GUYS WALK INTO A BAR, BUT THE THIRD ONE DUCKS.

760

How many tickles does it take to make an octopus laugh?

Ten-tickles.

761

WHEN A WOMAN IS GIVING BIRTH, SHE IS LITERALLY KIDDING.

762

A ham sandwich walks into a bar and orders a beer. The bartender says, "Sorry, we don't serve food here."

763

A string walks into a bar with a few friends and orders a beer. The bartender says, "I'm sorry, but we don't serve strings here."

The string goes back to his table. He ties himself in a loop and messes up the top of his hair. He walks back up to the bar and orders a beer. The bartender squints at him and says, "Hey, aren't you a string?"

The string says, "Nope, I'm a frayed knot."

764

Can February March?

No, but April May!

765

WHAT DID THE BUFFALO SAY TO HIS SON WHEN HE DROPPED HIM OFF AT SCHOOL?

"Bison."

766

Two peanuts were walking down the street.

One was a salted.

What do you call a cow with two legs?

Lean beef.

What do you call a cow with no legs?

Ground beef.

What do you call a dead fly?

A flew.

770

What is Beethoven's favorite fruit?

A ba-na-na-na.

771

Where did the college-aged

vampire like to shop?

Forever 21.

772

CASHIER: "Paper or plastic?"
DAD: "Either, I'm bisacktual."

WHAT DID THE HORSE SAY AFTER IT TRIPPED?

"Help! I've fallen and I can't giddyup!"

You know what the loudest pet you can get is?

A trumpet.

I hear it's easy to get ladies

not to eat Tide pods.

It's more difficult to deter gents, though.

776

What noise does a 747 make when it bounces?

"Boeing, Boeing, Boeing."

777

WHAT DO YOU CALL A FACTORY THAT MAKES PASSABLE PRODUCTS?

A satisfactory.

Waitress: "Soup or salad?"

Dad: "I don't want a SUPER salad,
I want a regular salad."

Did you hear about the circus fire?

It was in tents!

780

**You're American when you go into the bathroom,
and you're American when you come out, but do
you know what you are while you're in there?**

European.

781

**I'm only familiar with 25 letters
in the English language.**

I don't know why.

782

**A woman is on trial for beating her husband
to death with his guitar collection. The
judge asks, "First offender?"**

She says, "No, first a Gibson! Then a Fender!"

WHAT DOES AN ANGRY PEPPER DO?

It gets jalapeño your face.

What does a nosy pepper do?

It gets jalapeño business.

As a lumberjack, I know that I've cut exactly 2,417 trees. I know because every time I cut one, I keep a log.

786

Did you hear the one about the bed?

No? That's because it hasn't been made up yet!

787

What do you get when you cross

an elephant with a rhino?

Elephino.

788

I WAS INTERROGATED OVER THE THEFT OF A CHEESE TOASTIE.

Man, they really grilled me.

What happens if you rearrange
the letters of "Postmen?"

They get really pissed off!

Did you see they made
round bales of hay illegal in
Wisconsin?

It's because the cows
weren't getting a square meal.

791

WHAT DO YOU CALL A LONELY CHEESE?

Provolone.

792

Dad (to a singer): Don't forget a bucket.

Singer: Why?

Dad: To carry your tune.

793

I told my 14-year-old son I thought "Fortnite"

was a stupid name for a computer game . . .

I think it is just too weak.

794

How do you make a Kleenex dance?

Put a little boogie in it!

795

WHY DID THE FARMER GIVE THE PONY A GLASS OF WATER?

Because he was a little horse!

796

Nurse: "Blood type?"

Dad: "Red."

797

I heard Youtube, Twitter, and Facebook are all merging. They're going to call it You-Twit-Face.

798

I tried to get reservations to the library, but they were completely booked!

799

A TERMITE WALKS INTO A BAR AND ASKS, "IS THE BAR TENDER HERE?"

How do you find Will Smith in the snow?

You look for fresh prints.

Studies show that cows produce more milk when farmers talk to them.

It's a case of in one ear and out the udder.

THE INVENTOR OF THE THROAT LOZENGE HAS DIED.

There will be no coffin at his funeral.